BOSS MOMS

JESUS, COFFEE, & PRAYER
Christian Publishing House

You Can Have It ALL With Christ!
Presented by The Q.U.E.E.N Xperience Founder
Min. Nakita Davis
~Queen Collaborative~

i

Copyright page

For permission requests, write to the publisher, addressed "Attention: Permissions Coordinator," at the address below. www.jesuscoffeeandprayer.com Presenting Author: Min. Nakita Davis jesuscoffeeandprayer@gmail.com – Publishing House Publisher: Jesus, Coffee, and Prayer Christian Publishing

400 West Peachtree Rd. NW STE 4-5055, Atlanta, GA 30308 www.jesuscoffeeandprayer.com

Cover/Chief Editor: Jesus, Coffee, and Prayer Christian Publishing House LLC

ISBN: 978-1-952273-03-2

Table of Contents

DEDICATION

This book is dedicated to All my Boss Moms across the Globe!

You are loved and Your tireless work to raise the next generation does Not go unnoticed!

In Loving Memory

Loretha Willams

Boss Mom to Queen Co-Author:

Dr. Tonya B.

NOTE FROM THE PUBLISHER OF PURPOSE

#jesuscoffeeandprayer

Queen,

Thank you for choosing to embark on a journey of wisdom, transparency, and loving inspiration towards your GREATER!

My deepest desire as the publisher is to Magnify God, bless You (my Tribe) in any season, and give hope to raise your children while #SecuringtheBank!

In these modern times, you can never get enough encouragement, positive affirmation, and tools to equip you to Win in any season of life.

As a Boss Mom to two fabulous kiddos, I too, know the uphill battle and yearning to love on your kids and family, all while loving on yourself and the God-Given Dreams *gifted* by our Almighty!

The Struggle is real… but our God is the realist!

Be encouraged in this season and know that your Gift Will Make Room for YOU- When You make room for it.

Now more than ever, I have learned to love harder, laugh more, praise my Lord and Savior~ Jesus Christ MORE, and to relentlessly pursue my DREAMS. Each day, I'm learning and growing while teaching my babies- that All things are possible through Christ.

From One Boss Mom to Another- know that I AM Proud of YOU!

God Bless & Enjoy #BossMoms

Min. Nakita Davis
Founder & CEO of
Jesus, Coffee, and Prayer Christian Publishing House LLC.
www.jesuscoffeeandprayer.com
The QUEEN Xperience platform &
Women Win Author & Business Summit

Dr. Tonya Blackmon

WE ARE WOMEN OF WEALTH

"She considers a field and buys it; out of her earnings, she plants a vineyard."

Proverbs 31:16 NIV

"She sees that her trading is profitable, and her lamp does not go out at night."

Proverbs 31:18 NIV

Are you a Boss Mom?

Defining aspects about a Boss Mom can be challenging because boss Moms are people that come in many sizes, shapes, and from all ethnic groups. A Boss Mom can be a single or married woman who has birthed or adopted children. Boss Mom's value motherhood. They face unbelievable challenges, many times in secret. They know how to make $25 worth of food stretch until the next payday.

Boss Moms understand financial terms, like REIT investments, monetization, collaboration strategies, streamlines of income, flipping homes, side hustles, trust funds and etc. They have earned the title "Boss Mom."

Please allow me to brag about 'MY MOM' (Mrs. Loretha). To me, she is the epitome of a Boss Mom for so many reasons. As I sit and create this chapter for you, I am traveling to see her, because she was diagnosed with a life-threatening illness over a year ago. The tone in my sister's voice suggested that I hurry home. Through tear-filled eyes, I will share some of my Mom's story and our journey. It pains me to know that when this book is published, she will not be here to read it.

Listen, even though I have earned a Doctorate in International Business, my greatest teachers have always been my mother, two grandmothers (Ruth & Ruth Mae) and great grandmother (Florrie Mae). All four of them planned, started, and grew successful businesses. I thank God that I was there to glean.

Boss Moms are made!

Experiences like this COVID-19 global pandemic has a way of making us rethink our values and goals. Trauma and uncertainty tend to lead us in a positive or a negative journey. I would love to tell you that I started my business because I had a moving epiphany. Truth is, my husband and I were experiencing marital conflicts that we both were sure to end in divorce. But God knew better! By the way, we just celebrated 28 years of marriage. Sis' listen, when you are facing difficulties, choose the positive path.

Let me get back to why I started my business. Because of a military move, I resigned from my $44 per hour job and moved where my husband wanted me to be, and I ignored what God had led me to do. It is was no surprise to me when I woke up one day and saw that my personal finances were in the red. I had put myself in the place of lack. So, I decided to start a business that same day. By the end of the day and by God's grace, I had earned my first $250. That was 10 years ago, and today I have the honor of still serving that same client. Choose the positive path, Sister!

I can hear your questions. How am I going to start a business with no capital? Do I know enough to be in business owner? Do I have to quit my current/quarantine job to be in business? Who will cook, clean, and take care of my Bae-Bae kids (just kidding) while I work this new side hustle? Here are some answers-

- You do not need $1 to sell your expertise as a consultant using the free Zoom app.
- You are beautiful, smart, the bomb.com , and valuable!
- No need to quit your day job- plan and do your business during lunch and 30 minutes each night before going to bed.
- After your business plan is done, share it with your children & then delegate their future roles in your family business. Frequently, discuss your ideas with them. (NOTE: The first time my son watched me earn $1,000 in one day greatly influenced his way of thinking about money.)
- Just do it, Sis! If you need help or have questions, just reach out to me! I was born to help Boss Moms manifest their true wealth.

Do you believe in God?

If so, know that he owns the Earth and everything in it. So, when you sit and start planning your wealth-building strategies, write it out (step-by-step), knowing that God will provide what you need to build your business. Disclaimer: nothing just appears. You will have to detox from Netflix, work your plan when you can, educate yourself, and have the courage to take the risk. To open a fish market, my Boss Mom (Mrs. Loretha) used $2,000 credit card debt to buy the food to sell in her new business. Next, she and my Dad eventually bought the restaurant and opened another business. Even though she did not have a cosmetology license, she used dedication, hard work, negotiation skills, and business acumen to grow a successful salon business.

Furthermore, my great-grandmother (Florrie Mae) and grandmother (Ruth Mae) were my first employers. My siblings and cousins helped our grandparents cater food, clean homes, and churches. We learned how to negotiate prices and use our skills to earn money. Quickly, we learned how to do our best even when nobody was looking. Remember, it is up to us to teach our children how to create and keep wealth, not the educational systems.

Distractions Alert!

Remember, Boss Moms are divinely made. Let us be truthful. Like me, you have many responsibilities and roles in your home, church, community, jobs, and/or CEO of your businesses. Being a Boss Mom can be one of the most rewarding and hardest jobs in the world. There have been times that I feel like I am being pulled in multiple directions. How do I maintain balance? God's word encourages us to do everything decently and in order. So, I stick to my schedule. I conduct calls 2 days per week, only accept up to 2 speaking engagements per month, and limit my client load.

Most importantly, I schedule exercise, prayer, cooking, vacation, and family time. It took me an extra two years to complete my doctoral degree. I cannot blame anybody because I allowed distractions from all around me to distract me. Once I set boundaries, I finished. Getting off schedule may happen, so start the next day again. I give you permission to begin again, Sis.'

#BossMomTips

- Know God for yourself (Pray, Worship, Listen, Record & Obey)

. . . but the people that do know their God shall be strong and do exploits. Daniel 11:32b

- You are Valuable!

Begin a Boss Mom means asking yourself the tough questions:

What do I love doing?

How much money do I want to earn?

Will my current skillsets help me reach my financial goals?

Do I need to finish a degree, earn a certification, and/or hire a mentor?

- Create a personal plan and a professional business plan **(Connect with me for help with this.)**

Trust in the Lord with all your heart and lean not on your own understanding; in all your ways submit to him, and he will make your paths straight. Proverbs 3:5-6 NIV

- Share your dreams with your core group and get their feedback.

Children are a heritage from the LORD, offspring a reward from him. Psalm 127:3 NIV

- Create a Contingency Plan for your personal and professional goals.

In other words, what would happen if you lost your job, got a divorce, or your current stream of income stopped? Develop a plan to meet those needs. (**Connect with me for help with this.**)

Lazy hands make for poverty, but diligent hands bring wealth. Proverbs 10:4

My Prayer

Dear God,

I stand in the gap for the reader of this book and everyone that is connected to her. I decree and declare that Psalm 91 and the blood of Jesus covers them. No weapon formed against them shall prosper. You have placed specific gifts, skills, and talents in your daughter. I ask that you move by your Spirit to surround her with people, resources, favor, and strength to create and grow wealth. Although we are going through the pandemic, we are positive, strong, and on fire for Jesus. We have the mind of Christ. Help us to turn trauma into triumphant victories. I call her forth as a wealthy (body, soul, and spirit) Boss Woman in the Kingdom of God and the marketplace!

In Jesus name,

Dr. Tonya, B.

About the Author:

Dr. Tonya B. is a Veteran, consultant, podcast host, grant writer, sought-after speaker, and 2x Best-Selling Author. She inspires and educates Big businesses to achieve their dreams by developing strategic plans, in-depth research, and leveraging her wealth of knowledge. She holds her PhD in International Business Studies.

www.congempowerment.biz
https://linktr.ee/drtonyab7
https://bookme.name/TonyaB/lite/7
https://www.instagram.com/drtonyab_live/
www.linkedin.com/in/dr-tonya-bl
https://coursecraft.net/c/drtonyab/splash

Tekeisha Wade

THE HEALING OF MY SOUL

Do everything in love.

1 Corinthians 16:14

Be still, and know that I am GOD. I will be exalted among the nations, I will be exalted in the earth!

Psalm 46:10

Obstacles/Hardship: I felt that I was always chasing and running after an unknown tension. It led to feelings of loneliness. I thought a false reality would become my reality, so I started seeking the unknown tension.

I grew up in the church, but I was never taught the Biblical order of building a family. Meanwhile, the pain and the hurt I felt within my inner child were never healed. The inner child was trying to make grown decisions. Therefore, the building of my family was developed in a worldly way.

The journey began with my 1st born.

I was so excited that I was having my first baby, and finding out she was a girl was more exciting. I was beginning to feel fear overcome me because, at the time of discovering I was pregnant, I was unemployed. I started to worry a lot, but I began to use the worry to push me. I was on a mission. I started applying for jobs that would put me ahead financially. I was so excited when I got the call to come in for an interview. I went to the meeting and was hired on the same day. However, some problems began to arise.

I had suffered a bad break-up right before the pregnancy and wasn't truly over the relationship. Instead of grieving the relationship properly, I decided to enter a new relationship shortly after. I wasn't thinking; clearly, I just wanted to get over the pain. As soon as I started to settle into the new relationship, my ex decided he wanted to rekindle the relationship. I still had feelings for him, which prompted me to think about moving back into the relationship. But there was one problem, I was in a new relationship with a guy that I had grown to have feelings for. Upon making the final decision, that was the point of me finding out that I was pregnant. I felt the excitement and fear at the same time because the feelings of confusion began to set in. Here I am, pregnant by my new boyfriend and making the decision to go back to my ex. My thought process was, Oh my gosh, what will my ex say and will he want to be with me after telling him that I am pregnant by another guy. I felt like I couldn't take that chance. I let the new guy know that I was pregnant, and he was also excited. I told my ex that I was pregnant, but there was one problem I told him I was pregnant by him.

I carried this secret for years.

I knew in my heart that this was wrong, but being selfish and wanting what I wanted, I kept the secret safe. I even kept it from my daughter.

This was a dark moment in my life.

As time moved on, I decided to do a restart of my life. Once again, I did not heal properly from the previous relationships, yet, I met a new guy that became my husband. We had three children together. My pregnancy with my second child was high risk. The placenta was slowly detaching, causing me to go on bed rest in my 1st trimester. I had so much fear that I would lose her. The days were long and lonely during my pregnancy. I suffered depression, homelessness, mental and emotional abuse during this pregnancy. I found myself stuck in a cycle of pain and disappointment. My husband was my fiancé at the time, and the relationship was up and down like a rollercoaster. The times I needed him the most, he was not there. The lonely nights consisted of constant crying. I would reach out and get his voicemail. He was operating on his own time.

With the complications of the pregnancy, I had frequent visits to the hospital. I had to be in the hospital room alone. The constant attention-seeking prompted me to act as a private investigator by searching for answers on my own. The saying is, If you search for something, you will find it. I sure found what I was looking for. He was engaged to me and another relationship with someone else.

I was devasted.

In my mind, being pregnant would change him or draw us closer. I confronted him about it, but the cheating continued. I felt like I was constantly preaching to the choir by telling him how this hurts me. No matter how I looked at it, I loved him, and forgiveness kicked in. Months later, we said, "I Do." Within our marriage, I became pregnant with my son. The joy I felt was indescribable. My husband was with me during and after the delivery, what more could you ask for. I came home with my baby boy, but the joy I felt would soon fade.

The emotional and mental abuse became worst.

I kept asking myself what I did to deserve this. I started calling out to GOD and JESUS. I just wanted the pain to stop. I would sneak in the room and pray over my husband as he slept. I wanted him to change. GOD answered my prayers. But it wasn't the answer I was looking for. When my son turned 6 months old, my husband left me to be with someone else.

Again, I was devastated.

I felt like I wanted to die.

That is when I started seeking GOD more and slowly moving toward my passion, Singing, and Songwriting. I started focusing more on the kids and providing for them. I lost focus after being in a vulnerable state of mind, and that's when we reconnected. And that's when I got pregnant with my 4th child.

This was a long story short.

I wanted to begin by sharing with you some of my adversities.

My story did not end there, it was only the beginning.

GOD began performing surgery on me mentally and emotionally, including the matters of my heart. The places where the abuse penetrated. I could not have done it on my own. I had to learn to Surrender and push myself to the next level. My next level was the push to my new home, Minnesota. It was a thousand miles away from the state I was born in. I must say that this move came with me being obedient. When I made the decision to move, GOD moved swiftly. I started my new job and moved into a beautiful new home in the country. The kids were so happy. One night I couldn't sleep and utilized that time to think. GOD put on my heart to enroll back into school. I was unsure if I should continue to study the HealthCare Administration or move into a new major. Within several weeks, I started to tune into Periscope. Upon watching a Life Coach and Counselor caught my attention. After listening to her for several weeks, GOD put on my heart to enroll in The Coach Training Academy. I did doubt myself; however, I had to push myself out of my comfort zone. So many doubts came into my head, especially being a single mother of 4 children. I obeyed The Lord and enrolled; therefore, I joined in with the kids when the kids studied and completed homework. As they saw me studying, completing homework assignments, and listening to lectures, it pushed them to work harder on their schoolwork.

I had to pray for balance to work a full-time job, attend classes, and be a mom.

I prayed for balance daily, and GOD provided the balance.

I was able to level up while being a mom.

I would assign the kids chores to assist around the house and other tasks to limit the overwhelmingness. During this time, I made a significant decision to Love Me Better. This consisted of building a stronger relationship and bond with The Lord, practicing self-care, and having a healthy relationship with myself first. I dated myself, hired a Business Coach, started my business, and made an appointment with a Therapist/Counselor. However, it was and still is a process.

I had to learn patience during this time and trust the process. It took a lot of prayer and Faith as well because it does not happen overnight. Having Faith is what kept me grounded. With Faith and Hope, GOD provided me with many resources and support, such as reliable childcare with the help of my oldest daughter. At one point, my mom came along to help. My ministry came to light through a Vision from GOD. He used my Business Coach/Consultant to bring a prayer to me. Upon praying the prayer, GOD gave me the vision within 5 minutes. I saw the silhouette of a man. I met with my Business Coach, and we put our heads together, and the vision GOD brought to me was being a Life Coach for Men. I was able to narrow down my niche by the time of graduation.

My journey consists of first and foremost building a healthy relationship with Christ and Self. Breaking unhealthy patterns, healing, practicing Self-Care including recognizing, building and maintaining healthy relationships, and looking in the mirror at Self. It starts with a Prayer life and dying to self on a daily basis. We all must learn how to Pause and Focus on GOD and Purpose. As a Woman of GOD and Mother, I had to learn to Pause and Focus on my mental and emotional health, including Self-Awareness. These elements are essential. I had to learn to keep my eyes on GOD and Surrender completely. I had to allow him to fight my battles and know that I have the Victory with his help. Once again, Obedience is key. I am overcoming by practicing these steps. Everyone has their own story, Purpose, and BluePrint. Our journeys will be different; however, we will come out as Winners.

We will be Fireproof.

We must vow not to live in our mistakes and bad choices. This was part of the plan; therefore, we must dust ourselves off and get back on track. Every day is a learning experience because we are not perfect. Through my life experiences and lessons, I am now an International Certified Relationship, Men's Empowerment, and Leadership Coach. Also, an International Speaker, Singer, and Songwriter. Even though I did not get to experience, during my first part of the journey, a man/husband nurturing me during my pregnancies with healthy love. GOD is still brought me out with a strategic plan.

He does his best work in the dark.

Allow Him to work on you. I allowed Him to work and continue to work on me. If he did it for me, He will do it for you. Keep your head up because You are GOD's child, and you were chosen and created on Purpose.

GOD makes no mistakes.

I Love You.

Also, I am in the medical field, working frontline at a hospital during this time of the pandemic. I provide safety to our patients and support my community and children by staying in prayer and having an open-door policy. I provide hope with positive affirmations and by speaking too.

About the Author:

TeKeisha Wade, CRC, CLC is the Founder of Open Arms Connection LLC and EmpowerHIM Coaching, a life coaching practice/Ministry that's on a mission to empower, minister, and teach. She helps women and men move past their brokenness and renew their self-worth to a level where they see what GOD sees.

TeKeisha Wade is an International Certified Relationship/Men's Empowerment Coach and Leadership Coach. She is also a mother, International Speaker, Author, and entrepreneur. She has over 10 years of experience in Coaching and over 2 years of speaking. TeKeisha has experienced storms that brought her to healing, self-love, and putting GOD 1st place.

Yvette Simone

TRUST HIM, NO MATTER WHAT

Be anxious for nothing, but in everything by prayer and supplication with thanksgiving let your requests be made known to God. (NASB) -

Philippians 4:6 –

But the Lord is faithful, and He will strengthen and protect you from the evil one. (NASB)

2 Thessalonians 3:3

I have been young and now I am old, Yet I have not seen the righteous forsaken Or his descendants begging bread. (NASB)

Psalms 37:25

As a divorced mother raising a teenage daughter, life seemed almost unbearable. But with the help of God, we made it through. I raised a beautiful young lady who is unstoppable, independent, and determined to succeed. In 2011 my world changed when I was released from my job, my daughter was in her junior year of high school, and I was wondering how we were going to survive. However, God reminded me in his word that; "He would never leave us, nor forsake us," and that is when I learned to totally trust and depend on Him for everything! For many years I was a faithful servant unto the Lord and was taught to always give your tithe, talent, and time unto Him. There were times I didn't understand it all, but when 2011 hit, it all came full circle. That year was one of our best years. With no income, every bill was paid, we never missed a meal, and my daughter participated in every activity and school event she desired. There were checks in the mail; people were blessing us just because, and God's favor was all over our lives. It is now 9 years later and seems to be a movie in this pandemic, and God is still moving on our behalf. To all my #BOSSMOMS If God makes you a promise, trust Him that it shall come to pass. Be obedient to God and His Word, and He will see you thru. Don't worry about anything; instead, pray about everything. Tell God what you need and thank him for all he has done.

About the Author:

Yvette Simone is an ordained Elder, Worship Leader, Psalmist, Motivational Speaker, and National Recording Artist. She is the proud mother of one daughter, loves working with youth to encourage them to become whatever they desire. She has been thru many trials and tribulations of Life's Journey, but she continues to trust God thru it all. Her current single "Won't He Do It' is a testimony of how good God is!

Website: www.yvettesimone.org
Facebook (Personal Page): YvetteSimone
Facebook (Artist Page): Yvette Simone Project
Instagram: YvetteSimone
Twitter: YvetteSimone01

Myechia Barnette

BUILDING ABUNDANCE

11 For I know the plans I have for you," declares the LORD, "plans to prosper you and not to harm you, plans to give you hope and a future.

Jeremiah 29:11 (NIV)

13 I can do all things through [a]Christ who strengthens me.

Philippians 4:13 (NKJV)

My name is Myechia Barnett, and I am a mother of four children with one who is currently living with me. In 2009, I up and moved to Georgia, built on faith. I did not know where I was going to live, how I was going to get around, I just did it because I believe that God was leading me to do so. So, I left Chester, Pennsylvania, pregnant with my second son because I wanted to give them something better in life and new scenery. I also did not want them to grow up around sex, drugs, and money.

Within the years of me being on this Earth, I have been through a lot. Losses, bad relationships, trouble, divorced twice, prostitution, and so much more. On the flip side, God has brought me through it all time and time again. He has picked me up even when I did not deserve it and got myself into my own mess. God covered me when I went left when He said go right. (plenty of times) I am so grateful that He loves and forgives us despite ourselves.

Let us discuss my children. My grandmother on my mother's side passed away in 2016. From 2009 to 2016, my oldest son was away from his father who lived in Pennsylvania. So, while we were there, my son wanted to stay with his father. With tears in our eyes, I let him stay.

The decision was made with God telling me he will be alright and to trust Him. So, I did. I had two other children at that time.

I moved from place to place and stayed with a family member. Sometimes my decision making led to things.... consequences.

Long story short, my daughter was taken away from me while caring for her. Crushed, I did not see her or hear her sweet voice for one whole year.

Prayer, tears, and faith led God to bring her back to me.

Her father won physical custody of her in 2019. Although I was stable for 2 years, I was not making enough money to sustain her. Plus, I had a criminal case hovering over me as to why the judge did not grant me custody.

I must tell the Lord, thank you right now again because not only did the courts drop my charges, but it was entirely removed from my record too! God will do it!

Then we have my 4-year-old son now. A few months before I gave birth to him, my children and I were living with one of my aunts. I had just gotten out of a bad relationship and decided that it was time for a change.

I am not perfect, but I am a work in progress.

I recall, one of my children being negatively treated by other kids bear a location that we were temporarily staying.

I remember telling the child that was bullying my child to "Take your hiney back down the street before I knock on the door and get your mother!" (Maybe I didn't use the word hiney- but you get the picture.)

My aunt comes out of nowhere and yells, "Don't be cussing in front of those kids!" I was already building up negative energy from her trying to control me, and I went off.

I hollered, "Who are you to tell me what to say in front of my kids! They know not to cuss. You act like you never cussed in front of your children!"

The next thing I remember, I had the urge to hit her. She mentioned during the argument that my children and I had to leave.

She even started cussing...lol.

My newborn son was not that long ago born, and I packed my kids up and left. A friend of mine helped us get a motel room, and we had nowhere else to stay.

The room had bed bugs, and I just sat in my car with my kids and cried.

Boss Moms Move

For the love of my children, I swallowed my pride and asked her to take care of my children at least until I could get back on my feet.

Glory to God~ she did.

Despite our differences, my aunt has always been there for my kids... no matter what. That is a blessing for me, and I thank her for that.

I wanted my newborn to have a better chance, so I asked my close friend to take him in. She always wanted a baby boy, and, in the process, we were both blessed. He has a stable place to live, and financially, it was better for him, and as his mother, I trusted God. He is still with her till this day. My 10-year-old son is the one living with me. He is the one who moved to Georgia with me. He has no father or family in his life besides me.

In the past few months, I was working at a local supermarket, living with family, going to school from home, and building my businesses. While achieving all these things, praying, practicing the law of attraction, and helping people, God has blessed me day after day since the pandemic happened.

Last year, I lost my apartment, my car broke down, and I lost my job.

I am so grateful and thankful to God. He has been birthing so many things out of me during this time. I recently ranked up in both of my businesses, gained another business opportunity, and published two children's books on Amazon! I also have been blessed to meet Minister Nakita Davis in all of this. Her energy has given me the inspiration to keep going.

With all that being said, I want to thank everyone that has made an impact in my life. Whether good or bad, both have made me the woman I am today. Overcoming adversity, again and again, has enabled me to go even harder for myself and my kids.

I have grown mentally and spiritually through all of this. My future is looking even brighter by the second.

May God bless every reader!

About the Author:

Myechia Barnett is a great spiritual and inspirational leader. She always puts the needs of others before herself. She is a serial entrepreneur, business owner and author too! Her goal is to help as many families as possible to build a financially successful home-based business from home.

Dr. Lovella Mogere

LET GO OF THE DREAMS YOU'VE OUTGROWN

"He said to them, "Listen to this dream I had: We were binding sheaves of grain out in the field when suddenly my sheaf rose and stood upright, while your sheaves gathered around mine and bowed down to it."

Genesis 37:6-8

His brothers said to him, "Do you intend to reign over us? Will you actually rule us?" And they hated him all the more because of his dream and what he had said."

It's an age-old quandary: a loaded question that burns at the center of every human existence. "What do you want to be when you grow up?" We all want to know what others dream of becoming. Achieving. Owning. Conquering. Changing. Accomplishing.

We ask our children, 'What do you want to be when you grow up? We ask our impending high school graduates, 'What are your aspirations? What are your plans? What do you want to major in?'. We ask our siblings, our friends, our lovers – 'Where do you see yourself in ten years?'

Dreams provide a soul-feeding potion that we draw upon for initiative. The quest for more will have the heart yearning to show the mind at work in your personal and professional lives. It's a journey we're expected to embark on as soon as we're capable of cognitive thought. And we often just call them dreams. Because that sums up the growth and the more, but it adds passion and purpose.

Dreams are vital – it speaks of what you are most passionate about

I'm not telling you to stop dreaming for dreams are an intricate fusion of reality and the perceived future. They propel us forward. Dreams feed our souls as we draw upon initiative. We use them to shape our decisions, sometimes to the point of fixation and inflexibility. We know that achieving a dream involves focus and work. We know we cannot wish our dreams to fruition.

You need to hustle.

Sweat. Leverage inexhaustible drive. Keep your eye on the prize.

Dreams are also infectious. Your vision, having been expressed, becomes the ambition of the people within your circle. That's the signpost of a competent, supportive relationship, isn't it? Your nearest and dearest, standing tall in your corner and rooting you on. Sometimes, that exuberance fills us with the motivation to just get out there and chase that dream. And those dreams- they're also pliant. Meaning, what you dream of today, or ten years from now, is not, your magnum opus.

In a reflective view of the dreams fulfilled, my question to you today is this, have you surpassed those dreams? Have you transcended the mental timeline of your goals? As the carrier of your dream, do you think you have given yourself the time needed to implement the blueprint of the dream entrusted to you?

A dream you held in fierce exaltation three years ago may no longer call out to you in the same sublime voice. What feels like perfect truth yesterday may not be today. This is a side effect of your personal evolution.

Can you tell me right now that you are the same person today than you were a year ago?

How about five years ago?

What about ten?

As we grow older and sit more into our unique identity – our perceptions of the world (and ourselves) changes.

What do you do when your dream transcends beyond reality? The question posed, provokes thought, and as I think back, I saw myself running through loops of time, pursuing a dream.

Life choices, good and bad, have spiraled me in time. As I drew closer to achieving the dream, the narratives of a failed marriage, being a single mother of five, living on welfare, prompted thoughts of shame. The carrier of an idea is now a victim, for guilt became my language; it blinded the reality of my self-existence.

While on my journey to healing, it took me years to realize that my dreams and I, were not one.

I thought I was chasing a dream when, in fact, the dream chased me.

As I looked through the mirror of life, I realized that the voices of time lured me away from the path within the dream. Upon my spiritual awakenings, becoming one with time, my dream is now my reality. To my surprise, the dream I carried in seed form has grown past its infancy, adolescence stage, and now fully grown. As time dictates the path, I'm no longer the one who manifested the dream, but now the fulfiller of time called the dream. So whether that dream is still on your vision board or something you've grasped and lived, its magic may fade into the distance. This awareness can be disappointing. Even puzzling. Could it be that this is a sign for greater?

You may say this is all I ever dreamed of for my life. Why don't I feel the sense of contentment and completion I expected? Why am I intrigued by this path that leads in a different direction?

Could be that your core, the essence of you, is being stretched? Your dreams were meant to capture your attention!

Your dreams feed on your most profound thoughts for the survival of you.

Time has changed, you have changed, but you, and your exquisite journey of discovery, are not subject to boundaries.

What is your biggest fear in life, when your Dreams change?

But what do we do with those dreams? Those defined and individual yearnings of our hearts?

How do you digest a sense of betrayal against, well, yourself?

Who am I now?

What will I tell the most important people that are supporting me?

Do I have the courage to explain that I am envisioning something different for my life?

There is nothing wrong with saying goodbye to a dream you've outgrown.

It's OK to change career paths.

It's OK to walk away from an opportunity you were given.

It's OK to leave a great job and pursue a different one.

It's OK to take a hiatus from your professional field and explore a new one.

It's OK to pack up and move to another city, state, or country.

It's OK to shelf a goal and revisit it when you're ready.

It's OK to look at a relationship and say now it's time to let go.

It's OK to have different dreams, all occupying the same space.

It's OK to admit, to yourself, that your dream wasn't what you expected.

Our dreams are personal, and they serve us… Not the reverse. A dream, when the dreamer has abandoned their intent, it is meaningless.

If you are not inspired, why are you still in reckless pursuit?

The exceptional person you see in the mirror today was created, in part, by that dream. It cradled you and carried you into the now. What we seek in life should be an accomplice to our fulfillment – never an obligation. Joy is reflexive when you listen to your inner voice. Even when you're frightened. Even when that voice is in sharp disagreement with everyone else in your life, even when you want to ignore it and be a powerhouse of practicality. This puts me in mind of the story of Joseph, the scripture states that "Joseph had a dream, and when he told it to his brothers, they hated him all the more. 6 He said to them, "Listen to this dream I had: 7 We were binding sheaves of grain out in the field when suddenly my sheaf rose and stood upright, while your sheaves gathered around mine and bowed down to it." he saw and fulfilled the dream at the cost of losing those who disagreed with the dream. 8 His brothers said to him, "Do you intend to reign over us? Will you actually rule us?" And they hated him all the more because of his dream and what he had said. Genesis 37:6-8.

Though the voices of opposition will show its power, you must show the power within.

So, It's time to Release the dream.

Saying goodbye to a dream you've outgrown is a profound act of *courage*, and you have that boldness. You are under no obligation to fulfill a lifetime of dreams for anyone other than yourself. That includes paying dues to the distant past.

So in letting go, give gratitude to your dream. Take great pleasure in the ways it moved you. Ultimately, the exceptional person you see in the mirror today was created, in part, by that dream. It carried you at times, it resuscitated your heart, now you're like an immense river, cutting paths through the hard-shelled Earth to reach its destination. You're free to go. Valiantly, splendidly and honorably, don't allow your dream to keep you locked into a system when you were created to dominate the world. Queen, the world is your map.

#bossmoms

About the Author:

Dr. Lovella Mogere, is an entrepreneur, #1 best-selling author, and motivational speaker. She empowers women globally to live life intentionally by tapping into the power of intentional thinking. To learn more about Dr. Mogere visit www.lovellamogere.com.

Yolanda Jackson

SINGLE MOM JOURNEY

"God is not a man, that he should lie; neither the son of man, that he should repent: hath he said, and shall he not do it? or hath he spoken, and shall he not make it good?"
Numbers 23:19 KJV

"I can do all things through Christ which strengthen me."
Philippians 4:13 KJV

I remember when I first became a single mom in 2009. I never thought this would be my story. I grew up with a single mom until I was 11 years old. Soon I was placed into a children's home due to my mother's abusive behavior. My Mom had struggled with mental health issues all of my life. When I was taken away and placed in a children's home, it was the most peace I had experienced in a long time.

Later I was sent to live with my Great Uncle and My Aunt – who I now consider my Mom – and it was with them when I first experienced what it was like to have a two-parent home. I wanted to have that same lifestyle, and I made it my goal to have a marriage that remained a two-parent household.

This dream was not realized.

I got married to a man in the military, and we did not work out for multiple reasons.

When we separated in 2008, it left me raising two young children age 10 and 11 by myself. During this time, I left an excellent paying career to pursue my Master's degree before I knew my ex-spouse and I were headed for a divorce. Therefore, I had no income coming into the house except for what my ex-husband was willing to give me. I simply did not know what to do. I had a mortgage, two kids in private school, and a marriage headed for divorce at the same time. I was at my lowest point, a place I haven't been in for a long time. I did not know what to do except fall on my face and cry out to God. I heard him as I was crying out that He would get me through to the other side. He would take care of my children and myself. He will be my husband and a father to my children.

I could not see how this was going to happen, but He kept saying to me, keep your eyes on me. That is what I did. During this period, I was attending a church and was invited to a small women's group. In the group, the women encouraged me by praying for me. On one occasion around Christmas time, when I did not have any gifts for the kids, the women took me to a small room and said we want to bless you. They handed me a large sum of money. I refused at first because I had always been a giver during the time of my marriage. But they said, "Take it, just promise you will help other single moms when you come out of this situation." I made a commitment right then and there that I would help other single moms like myself if given the opportunity.

On other occasions, God would have people put money in my hand just because they were told by Him to bless me. During this time, God had me keep my children in a private school. This was not because of pride, but because my son needed a small school environment to learn and thrive. God in that provided for me to keep both my children in private school. He provided for me to keep my house. He also gave me a job, but the job at the time felt like a setback. I would sit at a desk in a Credit Union and greet people. However, God told me to treat this job as a high paying job. I did, and they gave me more and more responsibility. By the end of it, they were creating a job for me to work full time.

Also, God allowed me to stretch my unemployment by working part-time. Therefore it was able to last for almost a year. In the meantime, God was speaking to my heart to apply for a career that would change the course of my life. This job required me to have excellent credit and financial experience. My past job in Insurance, my Credit Union experience, military experience, and God was helping to maintain my credit history. I was able to apply for this career.

He had me turn down an opportunity presented to me by the Credit Union, He reminded me that it would not pay my bills and that this door was not Him. I told them and others that I could not take this job. People asked if I had another opportunity, and I said no, but God promises me that I would be working in this new career.

While I was waiting to hear back from this opportunity, it closed without anyone being selected. God kept saying to my heart, I will take care of your children and you. The opportunity reopened, I applied, I interviewed, and got the position. I knew that this is where I was supposed to work. However, even in the midst of this, I still had obstacles. I had to go off to training and had no family around to take care of my children. But God provided me with an amazing friend and sister who I was able to connect with, who took care of my children while I was gone. When I had to travel for my career, God provided people to assist me with childcare. It was not easy, but God helped me through it. He became my all and all. Everything He promised me began to come to manifest!

In the midst of this, God had me start a single mom's ministry in 2009, which I worked with two additional women from another church and touched other single Mom's lives. We were able to provide childcare, paper product needs, and even financial assistance. The ministry did well and ended in 2013. At the same time, God had me transition into a Women Director role around 2012 at a former church I attended. We were able to touch other women in the community. Later, I was ordained into the ministry in 2013 and continued to serve in that role until 2014. Afterward, God started to train me in 2015 to work with underrepresented communities and churches in the area of finances and compliance. I received my certification through AFCPE (Association for Financial Counseling and Planning Education).

In 2018, God started me along a path to work with compliance and finances within the church. I am currently serving as a Pastor at Force of Life International Church at Fayetteville underneath Senior Pastors Christopher Davis and Demetria Davis. At the same time, this church is overseen by Bishop Heanon and Nakeesha T. from Force of Life International Church. I serve on the board of Education Force of Life International and help churches in the area of compliance. My two children are in college, finishing up their last years. One is projected to graduate in December 2020 and the other one in May 2021. My ex and I have a working relationship. We can see beyond what happened in our marriage and make sure our children's well-being is first.

This time has not been easy, but God promises have come to past in my life. My encouragement to all single moms or parents when God makes a promise to you is that He will work out every circumstance for your good. He is faithful to fulfill His promises. I want you to also remember when the road is rocky, and obstacles seem impossible to overcome, that nothing is impossible for Him.

Your responsibility in this process is to trust Him.

About the Author:

Pastor Yolanda serves as a Pastor at Force of Life International at Fayetteville. She serves on the Board of Education for Force of Life International. She has assisted churches in the areas of Finance and Compliance. She is a single mother of two wonderful children: Israel Jackson and Bethany-Christine Jackson.

Charmaine Parker Lewis

CHECK YOUR ROOTS

"and provide for those who grieve in Zion - to bestow on them a crown of beauty instead of ashes, the oil of joy instead of mourning, and a garment of praise instead of a spirit of despair. They will be called oaks of righteousness, a planting of the Lord for the display of his splendor."

Isaiah 61:3 NIV

"The tongue has the Power of life and death, and those who love it will eat its fruit"

Proverbs 18:21 NIV

Mama! Mama!

Those precious words still ring through my home. My daughters are now 18 and 20 years of age.

The phrase they grow up so fast is purely authentic, and though I wish I could turn back the hands of time to slow it down so that they could remain, babies, a little younger, but what good would that do if I was the same person back then?

I taught my daughters not to allow the enemy to come in and plant seeds of death. His job is to kill, steal, and destroy. Use your God-given **authority** and speak life into your atmosphere.

Like those precious babies get older, we grow older. With age comes wisdom, character, wounds, maturity, and life events that will take us on the most perplexing rollercoaster. With that, we can share our experiences with our children or people that God may bring into our lives.

It's rewarding to share with others and say to them: "Hey, let me tell you what happened to me when I was younger."

So with that said, let me tell you what happened to me when I was younger.

I gave birth to two beautiful baby girls, one with smooth chocolate skin and one with a lighter praline complexion.

My skin tone isn't one that society would say is the most accepting because of the amount of melanin. I grew up with peers telling me that "you're too black, you're dark, but you're pretty, you need to go take a bath, and sometimes strangers would say this to me. Those words roasted in my head over and over daily, and they followed me into my adulthood. Words have so much **power!** The Bible states that life and death are in the power of the tongue, Proverbs 18:21.

One night, while in the tub, those words, like a magic trick, popped up in my mind, and drained down into my Spirit; it was like a scratched record or damaged CD.

"You're dirty."
  "You're too black."
     "You need to wash that dirt off."

In the past, I would have told you, I don't know what came over me, but as I stated before, with age comes wisdom and maturity. Now I know and understand that it was a spiritual attack on my life at a young age.

Even at birth, the enemy has plans to destroy the essence of your being because he knows that God has a purpose and a plan for your life, Jeremiah 29:11

Since young people's minds continually develop, it leaves room for the enemy to enter and ensure that negative seeds take root and grow spiritually as we physically grow.

One regretful night, while sitting in the bathtub, I did something that I kept a secret for a very long time. I attempted to wipe "dirt" off my skin or whatever contamination people thought was on my skin when they examined me. I was twelve years old when I sat in the bathtub and glazed over my skin; it was as if I was in a trans-state, out of body experience. Those offensive words just kept rotating in mind; you're too black, you're dirty. I started rubbing my wrist. Each time the words replayed in my mind, the harder I stroked until those gentle rubs turned into destructive scrubs. I figured in my mind; if I just kept rubbing, maybe the dirt will come off.

"I'm just dirty, keep rubbing it will turn lighter."

"Nothing is changing, I just have to keep rubbing."

Agitating my skin like that did not cause it to get lighter, but it did cause pain, broken skin, bleeding, and so I stopped and sobbed. I realized I couldn't change that about me, and I had no control over my skin color. I **accepted** the fact that it was something I was going to have to live with being dark. I became closed in, anti-social, I did not want to be around people, especially my peers. When I did go out, I didn't look people in the eyes. If I were in the store and saw a group of kids, I would go in another direction, thinking I'm not going to allow them to say anything about me. I wanted to stay in my room and write or build something, and I wanted to have control over something that belonged to me.

On the other hand, television shows, magazines, and music videos gave me another perspective of false beauty. From that, I began to measure myself up to other girls, along with being too dark, now I'm too fat, my hair is too nappy, I'm too tomboyish, and too this, and too that. I didn't realize how I allowed the enemy to go in and set up camp.

I did have a mother who was the "ride or die" type. She was and still is a well-respected figure in the community, and she was deemed the name gangsta' Pat from my husband. Mothers know when something is wrong. When I didn't come out of my room or was too quiet, she would see the droopiness on my face. Mom would ask that universal mom question, "Baby, what's wrong?" One thing about teens, regardless of how much your Mom tells you are **beautiful,** and you are **unique**; it's just not the same. You want to hear it from your peers; you want to be **accepted**, which wasn't the case for me.

So, the bashing of dark skin continued. I did make friends outside of my race; surprisingly enough, the discrimination came from the ones who looked like me. I believed maybe I was the ugliest thing out there, and that continued into my thirties.

God, some people act like they were the ones who created or molded me and colored me the wrong color. Lord, I'm exhilarated; you are the potter. Isaiah 64:8

In my youthful years, I was self-conscious about everything I wore, looked at me, my hair, acne, and boys. That's an entirely different story, one we don't have time for in this chapter.

Why this color out of all the colors on the melanin spectrum, why this end Lord? (*Uniquely made to fit God's purpose*).

My insecurities became an ailment because it started to affect me to the point where I felt I had to defend myself. My offense became my **protection**, and it grew roots and grew up with me into my adulthood.

Oddly enough, in my early twenties, I didn't want to date anyone my color or darker because I didn't want my kids to come out dark-skinned, I didn't want them to go through what I went through. If a guy looked at me, I would frown up quickly because, in my mind, I just knew he was looking at the color of my skin, and most of the time, that wasn't the case.

I met an awesome man of God, love him to life. When God blessed us with daughters, I made it a point to **speak life** over them, even while they were in the womb. I would always tell them how beautiful and intelligent they were and still are. I would make sure they heard it from their father also. My daughters help me to get over my insecurities. I had to show them that it is possible to succeed in life. I had to be an example, and I wanted to be their role model, not the television, not society. At the age of thirty-one, I decided to write a screenplay. My daughters were a little older, a little independent; therefore, I was able to do a bit more for myself. I entered my very first script competition and won. The smiles that grew across the beloved faces of my girls broke a lot of my insecurities. Right then and there, I knew writing was a part of my calling, and God gave me daughters to see true beauty, true love.

Still, today, when I walk into rooms, the 12-year-old me likes to come through, and that's when I have to be like a mom and raise myself. I have to tell her chill and grow up, girl, get over it. My daughters are older now, and they still watch everything I do, they are a **reflection** of me.

My love for **God triumphs** any insecurities I may have had. Now I understand when he gives you a gift to share with the world, share it. If you don't, it's disobedience, and I don't want to disappoint my father in heaven.

Steadily, speak life over your existence.

From ashes comes beauty!

Never let ANYONE keep you from doing what God has called you for because that very thing you are going through, someone else is waiting for you to tell them what happened.

About the Author:

Charmaine Parker Lewis is an award-winning screenwriter born in Baton Rouge, Louisiana. Parker Lewis has been in the film industry for twenty-two years and is the owner of DECODED Movies. She is an ordained minister under the teachings of Pastor Leslie Williams, and in 2015 she started a film club for the youth in her community. Lewis wants to do what God has planned for her and create life-changing stories and films that will alter the lives of many.

Social Media/Web
Website: www.decodedmovies.com
IG: Decodemymovies
YT: Parker Lewis The Writer
FB: https://www.facebook.com/profile.php?id=100010659391249
FB Pages: https://www.facebook.com/bittersweetchat/
Podcast: https://www.buzzsprout.com/989653/episodes
Linkedin: https://www.linkedin.com/in/parker-lewis-6038a110/

Evonn Firms

DEDICATION TO ALL SINGLE MAMAS

So the last shall be first, and the first last: for many be called, but few chosen.

Matthew 20 v. 16 KJV

"and who knoweth whether thou art come to the kingdom for such a time as this"?

Esther 4 v. 14

Wow!! Well, we've all had a moment in life where EVERYTHING CHANGED!! If we can be honest with ourselves first, of course, it was in that moment in life that caught us off guard and unprepared. Since I have extended the invitation to you ladies into a vulnerable place and space in my life, come on a ride with me!

My pegged quote, "man listen!!!"

When I separated from my ex-husband, my children were 8,6, and 4 years of age. Yes, hunni (honey), I had three youngins who witnessed the worst example of marriage for years! We behaved no better than them or their peers in our marriage at times.

YES, I was the product of a two-parent ministry AKA PKx2 (Preachers Kid to two parents), and he was the product of an intercessor. So both of us were raised and reared in the church. We knew the ways of the Lord but still found ourselves so far from God.

This sister had some significant decisions and moves to make.

While separated, I found myself unemployed. Unbeknownst to me, my ex decided to short-sale our almost two hundred-thousand-dollar home during this time too. To add insult to injury, he also had every utility service disconnected~ as everything was in his name.

Hindsight vision, listen, sista' girl, I can tell ya' that this shall never happen again!

I knew that God wasn't going to allow me to fall apart, although everything else around me surely was. I was in pieces, but I vowed to myself and Abba Father that my kids wouldn't be cut from the fragments of any of my perceived failures.

Roughly about a year after EVERYTHING CHANGED!

I began working on my first degree as a full-time business finance student. I started working a full-time job, all while being a full-time mother of three actively involved athletic scholars. My workday began around 5:30 am and didn't end until each child was supported! Glory to God, I didn't miss any parent-teacher meetings, games, or events, even in those times where I needed to attend multiple events at one time. Inevitably there were many days that I felt stretched thin trust me! After arriving home, preparing dinner, helping with homework, projects, baths, etc. this sista would be up until 3am in the morning doing my very own homework. By the time I closed my eyes, I would soon be awoken by my blaring alarm clock buzzing loudly at 4:15am.

I ran on fumes and faith during all of my children's days of youth. I always made it my duty to never allow my children to make me their God. As a mother, I lived by the fact that I still had to listen to someone; that no, I didn't get to do what I wanted just because I'm grown, and just because I'm the mama. I think as mothers (parents), many fail to realize that whatever life we create, whatever atmospheres we subject our children to. One thing is for sure what doesn't come out in the wash, it'll surely come out in the rinse. Unlike a laundry cycle, there are some things we shouldn't want our children to rinse and repeat.

Breaking Cycles

Raising prophetic children in a single-parent home is a task that many cannot say was or is easy. Really who can honestly say that you were taught how to parent effectively and efficiently as a single front?

Most of us were raised in the traditions of men, the traditions of the church, but not acquiring our own relationship with Christ. As a true mom boss of prophetic children, you learn to live what you are preaching! You realize that your relationship with God is just the example, as you raise and rear them to develop their own personal relationship with God. No you don't get to talk down, disrespect, their monetarily or physically unsupportive parent because you respect that your children's existence isn't just because of you sis! Abba has assigned you with the tasks of disciplining them and nurturing these gifts. For those of you who didn't correctly nurture your children's gifts, Sis, it's not over! Sis repent to Abba, Father, all is not lost! Seek to mend those relationships, and I pray that as you forgive yourself and take the initiative, that Abba restores and repairs you and your children's relationship.

Begin to Speak life into every area in their lives in which you may have spoken death...over their visions and dreams.

Oh, and forgive your ex too!

This is more than likely why you couldn't sow seeds of life because you were brokenly toxic. Break those cycles of those traditions that have held many of you captives to your own unfulfilled dreams. As many were taught that everything was of the devil. Break the cycle ya'll! Nurture and feed their visions and dreams. Cultivate them before you allow the people of this world to kill their hope! I knew Abba Father gave me three children in which all are athletic, but each with differing giftings within the prophetic. I thank God that yes, all three who are definitely, empaths. I know this doesn't register with most religious mindsets. I, however, had to allow God to guide me with how to nurture them. The calling upon my life, I can say, made it easier for me to relate to them and parent them both collectively and individually. When you know who you are and whose you are in Christ, it will help you to build and maintain a lasting relationship with your children. You will create a unique bond with your children that will challenge the old systems of my generation. "Do as I say, not as I do," will never get nor keep your children's respect for you as a mother.

I am so thankful that Abba Father chose me with my three gifts!

Overcoming Obstacles

Now I will be the first to tell you that baby, I have experienced many obstacles in my life. Listen, sis trust me I get it, I was the single Mom that couldn't get any help from the government. That alone taught me early that Abba was and still is my source. God wouldn't allow me to depend on NOBODY but Him. Today, my sisters stop expecting your help and support to come from those you thought would help you. At times, God will block folks from helping you, not because you're a bad mother, and He wants you to suffer, but because He doesn't want anybody holding nothing over your head.

God doesn't want anybody taking credit and stealing HIS glory out of your story! No, you're going to be LIVING PROOF, a credible witness, a bonafide walking billboard of what His favor really looks like! Sis many know your story, but they don't know half of the obstacles that you had to overcome. You are an overcomer!

Boss Moms Build From The Bricks

Build with every brick that's been thrown at you, boo!

My Lord, my bestie Lady is no longer here on Earth, but I can still hear her tell me that so clearly. So that's what I want to encourage you, ladies, on today with. Sometimes God will allow folk to throw bricks because they think it will deter you from reaching your goals, but they'll be used as a detour of building blocks to God's promises for your life. Keep building and keep stepping for every word spoken to defeat and destroy you; let it be the catalyst for you to everything they said you couldn't do! Open that business, write that book, establish that church, move to a new place, step out in faith, let every brick thrown make you BOLD in your walk and your faith.

Many of us look at the story of Esther from the surface level but walk with me into the deep for a minute. Esther 4 v. 14 "and who knoweth whether thou art come to the kingdom for such a time as this"?

I want to encourage you that NOW sis is your appointed time!

I don't care what your past looked like because I repeat- now is your appointed time. Everything you've encountered and you've endured Queen, you've passed the tests, you've survived things that would've took most slap out of here.

ARISE!!!

Like Queen Esther, she recognized her moment, and she seized her opportunity. I prophetically decree and declare that quarantine time was your preparation time. What most seen as "downtime" it was the time that Abba Father was advancing you. God is using everything the enemy meant for evil on your journey of pacing your floors and praying for your children. For every tear you shed when you didn't know how you were going to feed your children when you didn't know how the rent was going to get paid, He's going to turn it all for your good!

Congratulations, you've been anointed and appointed to recognize your moment and seize every opportunity coming to you! For such a time as this! Your math equation is not for those who can only do basic math.

Grind+Growth+Glow-No Losses=Multiple Wins!

Yes, sis NO losses just lessons!

About the Author:

Evonn is a proud mother of three young adults whom she attained two Bachelor's degrees while being a divorced single mother. She is a licensed and ordained evangelist who is gifted in the prophetic. This unique woman of God carries both a passion and a burden to help single mothers. She is the visionary and founder of two business endeavors: The Latter Rain Project, and inkNInspirations. She will be launching her ministry entitled Sister Keepers soon also!

Email: latterrainmovement@gmail.com
Facebook: Evonn Firms
Instagram: evrenee31
Twitter: Mpowrd2Npire
Website: www.inkninspirations.com

Sabrina Thomas

THERE IS HOPE FOR YOU

"Who can find a virtuous woman? For her price is far above rubies"
(Pro. 31:10).

"She looketh well to the ways of her household, and eateth not the bread of idleness. Her children arise up, and call her blessed; her husband also, and he praiseth her. Many daughters have done virtuously, but thou excellest them all"
(Pro. 31:27-29).

Becoming a pioneer or a pathfinder may be tedious, but becoming a path-follower should be the most natural thing for women of value. Mathematics tends to be one of the simplest subjects to record success because all you need to do is to follow examples. Similarly, I will use my multitude of experience as an entrepreneur, mother, woman of faith, and the magnitude of God's power to infuse hope into struggling women, mothers, business owners, and aspiring entrepreneurs alike.

Realistically, life is tough and turbulent. Regardless of your faith, age, gender, profession, position, or nativity, you will face challenges in this world. There is no time where parenting is easy; there is no place in the world where entrepreneurship is absolute; and no domain where faith is not tested. It is harrowing that women are the most vulnerable in our societies.

However, there is good news.

Jesus charged us to be of good cheer that He has overcome the world.

Again, whenever there is rage, don't forget that there is equally a range.

This implies that every problem has a solution; it has a limitation or expiration.

Life is spiritual, and achievement is divine. Therefore, it is impossible to sail or soar in life without spiritual support. Now, I will show you some secrets about my life. My anchor is "Godliness with contentment is a great gain." This is the fundamental principle of my life; it has helped me a lot.

The three steps of faith
- Godliness: This connotes an alignment with God. You need to be grounded in faith and advance in His knowledge. I'm what I am today by the grace of God. There is nothing that can grease your life like faith. You don't need to be downcast because your light will soon come. Your alignment will make you realize that you are not a victim but a victor.

- Contentment: This indicates a mental attitude. The condition of your heart is pivotal in all issues of life because as a man thinks in his heart, so he is – (Pro. 23:7). Similarly, as a woman thinks in her heart, so is she. The quality of your heart will surely determine the magnitude of your success. This implies that your life is in your hand because it is the picture in your heart. You can't think wrongly and live right. The direction of your thoughts will invariably determine the dimension of your life. Therefore, you should pay special attention to your mindset. The level of failure is proportional to the erroneousness of the mindset.

- Go for gain: Profit is the ultimate goal of any business organization or entrepreneur. Life operates on the principle of reward. People will reward you for the problem you solve. In contrast, God will reward you for the quality of your service to Him and humanity. Therefore, you must advance in every area of your life.

Wonders of faith

There is nothing you need that God cannot give you, and there is no mountain that encompasses you that God cannot surmount.

At this point, I want to reaffirm that you can be a spiritual woman of God, an excellent mother, as well as a successful entrepreneur.

If you still doubt yourself, remember that Christ is in you, the hope of glory. If you genuinely have God, glory is ahead of you. Moreover, your success as a boss mom is hinged on how you handle obstacles and eliminate negative thoughts. Ultimately you promote the positive life you desire to have.

Golden nuggets for boss moms

- Create time for yourself – success is impossible without taking time to create and develop it.
- Pursue your passion – it is your passion that will prompt you to wake up daily and tackle your life.
- Minimize your guilt – to advance in life, you need to silence the noise; you need to halt it.
- Exhibit financial intelligence – never spend what you don't have. Don't buy what you don't need with the money you don't have to impress the people you don't love.
- Set smart and uncomfortable goals – the only time you are truly growing is when you are not comfortable.

My Testimony

My life has not always been so rosy. I have stared the devil in his many times and told him, "Gods got my back!" He is the only one that can come through for me in such daring phases of my life. He always does.

Even though I work with parents of children and adults with different abilities, I don't hold back in letting my clients (parents) know my true story.

I am a mother to two lovely sons and a Grandmother (GiGi); my oldest is 25 years old, and the youngest is 19 years old. The birth of my second son, for me, I can say so far has been one of the toughest tests of my faith journey. He was born prematurely weighing just 600 grams; he was admitted to the hospital under intensive care for about four months. During those months, I prayed and cried out to God like never before. I knew I needed to believe in a power outside of myself, which is simply the power of the Most High God.

He came on oxygen, and a heart monitor, the first year, I prayed through that and had victory. After that, he was diagnosed with cerebral palsy, and like other times, I prayed through that and prevailed. Then, he was diagnosed with an intellectual disability, which I didn't hesitate to also pray about. Years later, he was again diagnosed with Autism, and I still prayed about that as well. In a nutshell, I shared my story so you can see that my journey has not been easy as a great mother, woman of God, and a faithful entrepreneur. Successfully enduring all of these obstacles has absolutely been because of God's Grace.

Throughout the journey of life, my faith has always been tested. It has always been struggling and battling, but I push through. So, in the last few years, I decided to become an entrepreneur. I started on my own spiritual journey because I know where my blessings come from. I know now that I can do all things through Christ who strengthens me. I know that I need God in my business to get to where I am going, which makes me now do things differently. No doubt that hard work, effort, and persistence are all important, but not as important as having that underlying belief that you are in control of your own destiny. There is a power in you that can make things happen, but all you need to do is recognize it and learn to ignite it.

I will lift up mine eyes unto the hills, from whence cometh my help. My help cometh from the Lord, which made heaven and Earth. He will not suffer thy foot to be moved: He that keepeth thee will not slumber **(Ps. 121:1-3)**.

As women of God, it is imperative to know that being in the most challenging, discomforting, and lowly positions in life are not enough to stop us from being hopeful.

In essence, it suffices to say that at every point in time of our lives, our hope should always be in God and in the fullness of what only He can bring about in our lives. That should always be our fundamental, not in man, influence, affluence, position, possessions, or whatsoever.

The LORD delights in those who fear Him, who put their hope in His unfailing love
NIV Psalm 147:11

As parents, we should consistently teach our children to see God as their source regardless of any privilege we can give them because this will help them early in their race of life to put their trust in God and not us – the parents.

Same goes for every one of us as a father, mother, wife, husband, chief executive, Pastor, or any title and we should not be carried away with what we have or have not as they are not the basis for the certainty of our tomorrow – our hope should be in God alone!

Let me end with this quote:

"When I stand before God at the end of my life, I hope that I would not have a single bit of talent left, and could say, 'I used everything you gave me" -Erma Bombeck

About the Author:

Sabrina Thomas is a Mother, Amazon Best Selling Author, Speaker, and passionate Autism & Special Education Advocate. She is dedicated to providing resources and tools to assist special needs families. Her mission is to ensure that special needs families achieve the best quality of life for their children and feel supported and empowered as parents.

Sabrina Thomas
Advocate.Speaker.Author
Email: sabrinatspeaks@gmail.com
Website: www.sabrinatspeaks.com
"Share Your Story, You never Know Who You Will Inspire."

Sheraton Gatlin

IT'S ALL ON PURPOSE

"Please, my lord," she said, "as sure as you live, my Lord, I am the woman who stood here beside you praying to the Lord. I prayed for this boy, and since the Lord gave me what I asked Him for, I now give the boy to the Lord. For as long as he lives, he is given to the Lord." Then he bowed in worship to the Lord there.

1 Samuel 1:26-28

"Do not worry about anything, but in everything by prayer and supplication with thanksgiving let your requests be made known to God. And the peace of God, which surpasses all understanding, will guard your hearts and your minds in Christ Jesus."

Philippians 4:6

With cameras flashing and big city lights, I moved to Atlanta, Ga. with a goal in mind. All I saw in my mind was one big word when it came to moving to Atlanta: an opportunity. I relocated from

Illinois to Tennessee, but still, I was craving just a little more. I always wanted to climb just a little bit higher. I was eager to move from Tennessee to Georgia. As soon as there was a job opening within my corporate job, I applied and took my chances to try something new.

I refused to leave Illinois without my only son by my side. I just couldn't see leaving him behind. And through thick and thin, he rode it out with me. We moved from Illinois to Tennessee and from Tennessee to Georgia, where I figured I would stay put for a while. Moving to Atlanta was a goal I had in mind for quite a while. After specific life experiences and obstacles, you grow, and you learn.

I learned enough and went through enough. It put a fire under my behind and inspired me to go after my dreams! I wanted to build a better life for my son and me.

Moving away from your family, especially as a single mother, can be a tough thing to do and a tough decision to make. Having family and friends support is why many are afraid to step out of their comfort zone or relocate. As we all want someone trustworthy watching over our children, and it feels good just knowing when your support system is secure and has your back. It can become hard to decide on taking a risk.

When I moved to Tennessee, I prayed and asked, "Lord, please help me find someone to help me watch over my son while I work." I prayed He would send me an angel, and He did. Through a colleague I met through my job, I was introduced to someone she knew could help me watch my son. They were a part of the same church family. I can honestly say I was blessed moving to Tennessee.

Moving to Atlanta, working a late shift daily, being a mom, and trying to adapt to a new city, life got busy. I was lucky I found a 24-hour daycare in Atlanta. However, I can't say my son was the happiest there. I would get off around eleven at night to midnight, and he was up waiting for me. Only for us to have to rush home, eat, and lay down, only to do the same routine the next day. My days off at the time were not weekends and holidays either, which made it even worse. It was definitely getting hard, and I knew at that age, my son needed a better schedule, the proper rest, attention, and the ability to be a child. As a mother, the best decision to make was to allow my son to go back and live with his father as he had been offering to help and wanting him to come back anyway. I agreed and figured this would give me time to get settled, work, save money, and prepare for my son to return.

While my son was away, I did not want him to think that I was living it up and had nothing to show for my move to Atlanta. I started trying to figure out what I could do to not only utilize my time and keep my sanity while away from my son, but also strive to build an empire.

I was starving for Success and bettering myself. I desired to leave a legacy for my son.

Success became my addiction.

I prayed, "Lord let me stand for something, so I just don't fall for anything. Let me have something to show for my time in Atlanta. I can't let my son down. If I can give back to him and my parents, I will be satisfied." It wasn't until later that I realized everything happens for a reason, and God is intentional as He allows things to happen that, in the end, work in your favor.

I am sure you know the saying, "be careful, what you ask for." Within eight years of living in Atlanta, I superseded every goal I had set for myself. "Lord Give Me Strength" became a frequent request of God from me. Wearing so many hats, daughter, mother, cousin, analyst, blogger, author, model, brand ambassador, friend, god sister, step-sister, where could I begin with trying to balance it all? But someway, somehow, He has kept me, and I keep on winning by his grace.

It certainly has not been easy. The decision to agree to let my son go back to Illinois alone took a toll on me. It took a minute to really pick my head up. I worked hard to work my way up the ladder and get promoted within my corporate job, to have a better schedule, weekends off, and to have my son return to me. As soon as I wanted my son to return, I was hit with a whirlwind. I had to go through court because my child's father felt differently about our son relocating back to Atlanta. I was completely caught off guard and felt defeated.

However, God had a purpose and a plan.

I am so grateful to God that He kept my mind. There were so many days I shed tears and wanted to give up. Still, I knew I had to fight for my son until the end, spiritually, emotionally, and mentally. I felt this was truly spiritual warfare, and the enemy would rather me be dead. From this mountain, I learned not only as a QUEEN but as a true woman of God.

I learned how to exercise my strength and POWER.

Although my son resides with his father, being a mom and bossing up can still be a challenge. It can also be emotionally and mentally draining as I miss my son daily. Many also assume since my son does not reside with me, everything is much more comfortable, but that is not always the case.

I do things to make balancing being a mom distant from her child easier and still maintain a relationship with my son. I find ways to relate to my son and engage him in conversation when we speak and spend time. I utilize technology such as video calling and communication via phone to ensure we stay connected. I am sure to be on the school's email distribution list, emailing his teachers at the beginning of the year and sending them a photo of me to identify who I am. I also log in to view his grades. When I am in town, I stop by my son's school to visit him in class too. At the end of the day, children remember the time we spend.

There are some strategies I use to keep me on track.

Prioritizing your day and time management plays a huge part in completing your day to day tasks promptly.

Being a boss mom can be overwhelming.

Prioritizing will allow you to boss up and be the best mom you can be. There are just not enough hours in the day, and there is too much to do to not have order or organization when there is a goal in mind to achieve. Personally, sis, I use my calendar like crazy. I set alarms too. Mental notes are good, but actually writing it down works better for me. I think ahead and decide what day of the week I can work on what project instead of trying to work on everything every day. I make time for friends and to be social and laugh a little as laughter is always good for the soul. When I feel like life is too much, a nice walk outdoors can always soothe me and bring me back to a happy medium.

I also invest in me.

I have a therapist that I see regularly.

It is always good to have a neutral party to talk to, someone that can provide you various perspectives on things.

I have incorporated meditation as well to assist in maintaining a clear mind.

I encourage you to go for your dreams and don't let anything stop you from bossing up but rather add fuel to your fire. Keep in mind that things happen on Purpose for a purpose. If you want it, you can have it this season. Keep the Faith, keep believing, and keep God first, knowing that everything happens for a reason. Anything that you need to fulfill your Purpose, remember God says, "I AM."

About the Author:

Sheraton Gatlin is a Published International Celebrity Makeup Artist and 3x Best-Selling author that continues to strive to fulfill her Purpose as a #BossMom. Wearing many other titles such as a brand ambassador, administrator, business owner, and firm believer, Sheraton is continually making her mark on the world. Her goal is to inspire others to do whatever God has called them to do. She is the epitome of, "if she can do it, I can too..." no limits, no boundaries.

VoirBelle LLC.
www.voirbelle.com
Instagram: @voirbelle
Facebook: VoirBelle by Sheraton

Rev. Tiffany Bellamy-Lyles

THE 9-5 MINISTERING MOMMA

*"But seek first the kingdom of God and His righteousness, and
all these things shall be added to you."*

Matthew 6:33 (NKJV)

*"Her children rise up and call her blessed; her husband also,
and he praises her:"*

Proverbs 31:28 ESV

Just like many of our modern-day women, I juggle many hats and
carry several titles. I'm an Ordained Reverend, 3x Best-Selling
Author, business owner, wife, and work in the corporate world of
banking. But most importantly, I Am Mom. I say being a mom is
most important because children are a gift from God. God
entrusted me to five children, and it is my duty to help build them
up to be upstanding citizens, husbands, wife, and most
importantly a woman and men of God.

This journey has been far from easy. I have had to quit a career to take a $10,000 pay cut to be able to work closer to home so I could be a present mom. I am a woman raising four sons and a daughter. The road sometimes is very rocky, and I don't always feel like I'm doing a good job. In fact, if I could be totally transparent, there are some nights I cry about that.

Being a mother, you are sometimes placed in positions such as doctor, nurse, chauffeur, banker, counselor, criminal defense attorney, prosecutor, nurturer, and the list goes on. Add working 9-5 for a well-known bank as a Team Lead and Minister to the equation, and there you have 'The 9-5 Ministering Mom.' I am asked often, "Tiff, how do you balance?" Truthfully, I sometimes have to sit back and ask myself the same question, but I know that it's nothing but God.

Before I get out of bed each morning, I read a Word from God. I start my day off this way to ensure my feet don't touch the floor until I hear from God. The enemy doesn't wait to attack, so I have to be prepared for the attack. Once I get up, I head straight into prayer. That time with God is especially important because I get to pour out my heart to Him with gratitude and praise as He pours back into me. Also, I get to receive directions and guidance for my day. After this, I make sure all the kids are ready for school, and my husband is prepared for work, and we head out for the day's adventure.

I work Monday-Friday, attend church Wednesday and Sunday, I have prayer night with my sister/prayer partner on Wednesdays as well. In between those times, I am ministering. Sometimes I can be on a prayer call anywhere between an hour to an hour in half. In between times, I'm cooking for my family and cleaning our home. I have a strong relationship with my children, so while I'm doing this, they are telling me their latest news or telling each other's latest news. No doubt, it gets very overwhelming at times. Plus, it's a must I have some quiet and intimate time with my husband. There are sometimes I need a second wind for the day. When I feel this way, it's a must that I seek God in prayer.

My favorite scripture happens to be Matthew 6:33 which tells us to seek first the kingdom of heaven and its righteousness and all these other things will be added to you. This helps me to shift my focus back to what God wants me to do. I know that if I look to Him to determine what's needed for the kingdom, He is going to ensure I have the needed strength to take care of all the tasks at hand.

If I could be frank, I have made many mistakes of being a mother. Sometimes it made me think that my kids would have been better off if they had someone else as a mom.

I learned that was a lie.

God knew all the challenges that would come with me being their mother, yet God still chose me to be their mother.

I realized that my children were not mistakes but rather opportunities, opportunities for me to grow. Opportunities for me to learn. With each opportunity came wisdom.

When my kids were younger, I didn't know how I would make it through, but we made it through, TOGETHER! I didn't just teach them, but they taught me too. They taught me how to really love beyond all faults and flaws. They taught me how to truly take care of others. They taught me how to be persistent, patient, and passionate. Most importantly, they taught me to never give up.

Being a wife, mother, 9-5 employee, and minister, while coming up with a business plan and strategy keeps me extremely busy and so fulfilled. The love and understanding that I get from my husband makes the load that much lighter. That brings me to this, being a single mother. I have been a single mother. Being a single mother places the weight of not failing even heavier on your shoulders.

I was always hard on myself because I worked so hard and spent minimal time being a present mother. Sometimes I would work 17 hours a day. That was until I learned that all the money in the world could not equate to the time I was losing.

God blessed me with less money but more time but eventually promoted me until I made more money and had even more time.

God is a rewarder when we take care of the things and people He gives us.

God sent me a husband who would help with the balance. Someone who understands that what God is calling me to requires me to help care for others that's not inside our home, which sometimes reduces the amount of time we spend.

Now with God increasing our territory, I'm working on some future endeavors that will ensure the wealth of my children's children and so forth. For years I stopped my life to raise my children. I soon realized that they will be out of the house in college, military, workforce, and someday married and raising their own children, and I'll just be here.

It was at that moment I decided to do things that would better me and prepare me for the journey of my life. God started to pour into me things that I loved growing up. The things that we often forget about due to the movement of life. One of those things was writing. I began to write and remembered how relaxing and exciting it was. I even began to love ministering because it helps heal people physically, mentally, and emotionally. It also heals the inner part of me that thought I could not be more than a wife and a mother. I thank God for renewed strength each day. The same way I begin my day is how I end my day meditating on the Word of God and prayer.

Finding Jesus was the missing piece of the puzzle because I'm able to do all things through Him. There are no limitations or restrictions in Christ. For that, I can keep going every day as long as my life is centered around Him.

I want to leave you all with a few helpful tips that have and continue to help me.

Start and end your day in the presence of God with prayer.

Know that someone else's perfect may not be your perfect, so don't compare or compete.

Manifest in the lane that God created for you and only for you.

Seek peace and pursue it.

Make time for what matters most, family, Live, Love, and Laugh often. Rest, not just any rest, but rest in the Lord.

Be thankful for all things.

Seek God first and find the good and everything.

Be patient. Our God is Always on time.

Glorify God at all times.

Seek to find favor with God and not a man because when you find favor with God He will make sure you find favor with man.

Nothing and Absolutely No One comes before God.

I rebuke any spirit of stagnation, procrastination, feeling like you're not enough, the spirit of I can't, excuses, fear, and intimidation. I declare and decree the Spirit of Power, courage, sound mind, I can, worthy, love, peace, and Success over your life. I speak God's blessing into your life.

To God, be the glory forever and ever.

About the Author:

Tiffany Bellamy-Lyles is a daughter of the Faith.

She is a loving mother and wife.

In addition to being a family woman and Christian, she is a 3x Best-selling Author, entrepreneur, Ordained Reverend, and works a 9-5. Rev. Tiffany does not only use these avenues to create wealth for her family but as opportunities to share the love of

Christ by finding ways to minister in all aspects of her life. The love of people is her passion.

Social Media Handles:
Facebook – Tiffany Bellamy-Lyles
Facebook – Tiffany Bellamy-Lyles Sharing Christ
Instagram – rev_tiffanyblyles

Lowanda Davis

DON'T WORRY~HE'S GOT YOU!

Don't worry about anything; instead, pray about everything. Tell God what you need, and thank him for all he has done.

Phil 4:6 NLT

Is 54:17 KJV
But in that coming day
no weapon turned against you will succeed.
You will silence every voice
raised up to accuse you.
These benefits are enjoyed by the servants of the LORD;
their vindication will come from me.
I, the LORD, have spoken!

I became a mother on January 3, 1996. It really was a different kind of day for me. To think back on what my feelings were that day, I must say nervous, scared, happy, and excited, just to name a few.

Motherhood was something different that I had never experienced, and I was uncertain I could do this. However, it was way too late to change my mind, right? Well, as the years went by, I got divorced and had to care for this little person all by myself.

What am I going to do?

I cried many nights scared and unsure I was doing this the right way. I was a US Army soldier and didn't have any family in Germany, so who could I turn to? However, even though I wasn't saved I did know about the Lord as my Mom and Grandma made sure of that (Prov 22:6). I knew I'd need His help on this special journey.

I must tell any mom reading this that depending on Jesus was the best decision I ever made.

I began to cast my cares upon Him because I knew He cared for me.(1 Pet 5:7 KJV) I stopped worrying about things I had no control over and prayed more (Phil 4:6 NLT) I knew that no matter what people tried to do or say, I could make it because He loves me. (Is 54:17KJV) When we as mothers actually read the word and do as it says, we will find that raising children can actually get better. We read Proverb 22:6 and stop there but one of the most important verses comes a little further in the chapter. Verse 15 is an awesome scripture (read the NLT). Now for those that don't want to discipline their children well, that's on you.

After reading that scripture and putting it into effect, my life changed. Let me make it clear that I didn't abuse my child, far from that. When she was just 1 yr old, if she touched something she shouldn't have, I very lightly spanked the hand she touched the item with. She didn't cry because I didn't mean to make her cry; I only wanted to get the point across that she shouldn't touch that item.

IT WORKED!!!

I kept that going until she was around 3yrs old. Very seldom did I have to spank her for anything twice. Small children learn fast!!! So fast forward to 12 years later, I had a well-mannered child that was adored by many. Now some years later, she's 24 and still respectful. She's not perfect, but she is the result of a Prov 22:15 child.

Being a Boss Mom can be tranquil when you have the right strategy and the right motivation. My daughter is grown now, but when she was living with me, and I had to work, we were a team. I know some of you have more children to raise, and it's not easy, however, when you train them all in the fear and admiration of the Lord, it'll make a difference in everything. Working hard and pushing forward gets easier when you know that God is in control. No one can bring you down unless you allow them to. As long as you can pray, you can WIN!

All of this is my experience and what worked for me as a single parent.

Now, if you are married and have a great helpmate, then that's a plus. Two parents practicing Prov 22:6,15 are better than one. However, to my single moms, I say push forward be what God has called you to be, and let us make Boss moves in a new season. Always know that you Don't have to Worry, He's Got You!

About the Author:

LoWanda "Dee" Davis is a Woman of God, Veteran, Playwright, serial entrepreneur, and 2x Best-Selling Author. She is a blessing to many that she encounters

Hazel Elaina

TINY TRAVEL AGENTS

"Delight yourself in the LORD, and He will give you the desires of your heart."

Ps. 37:4

"The thief's purpose is to steal and kill and destroy. My purpose is to give them a rich and satisfying life."

John 10:10

It was June 2019, and I was the music director at my church in North Charleston, SC. My Pastor approached me about revamping our dormant children's choir during the summer. As a music teacher with 11 years of experience, I was glad to do it. My kids were already coming to church with me. At the same time, I served as a music director, bible study leader, and intercessory worship leader, so adding an additional leadership role felt normal.

I enjoyed seeing them sing with microphones instead of having their eyes glued to their tablets during rehearsal. To break the ice, I simply asked, "How is everyone starting off their summer break?"

The other kids gave the usual answers: eating out, going to the movies, sleeping in, and chilling at home with their siblings. My daughter raised her hand first, but to avoid showing partiality, I chose her last. My daughter said, "My family is going to Miami this summer!" She expressed a huge smile with pride in her eyes. Her brother beamed with joy next to her. I looked at her in shock and said, "I don't know how you're going to get there! Do ya'll have Miami money?!" Their faces looked like their soul was broken, and their dream was crushed. Sadness loomed in their eyes, and they slowly put their heads down in shame.

There I was, a college-educated woman of God, anointed, prophetic, talented as a pianist and passionate as a singer, but of little faith. I had over 20 years of experience serving in ministry as a preacher's kid in high school, all through college, and into my middle-age years. Still, I only applied faith to the spiritual aspects of my walk. My children were literally standing in the pulpit, declaring their faith to go visit my family in Miami, Florida. Yet, I spoke to them just like the Sanhedrin's spoke to Jesus.

As we drove home that night, I realized that my lack of faith stopped me from driving home every summer. I hated the holidays because I never saved up enough money to visit my family. I had to pretend to enjoy hearing colleagues share their "went to see family" memories when we returned to work. The Covid-19 quarantine was like my usual vacation: I was stuck at home with no place to go, wishing I could get out and go everywhere. My shelter-in-place orders were voluntary, doubt driven, and took place every winter, spring, and summer break for eighteen years. And to make matters worse, one of my fellow teachers planned a "Girls Trip" to my city, with almost ten cousins and friends, while I struggled to get my family of four down there. I had a pattern of going home every three years because that's how long it took me to get unbearably homesick.

That night, I stayed up late and began to brainstorm ways to get back home. One of my ministry friends was a travel agent, and she gave me a link to a discount hotel website that she no longer used. And I made sure I took my kids to Miami that next month. I told my sister, "I am coming back this summer, and I am living like a tourist when I get there!" And we did. I found a beautiful condo near Collins Avenue in the prestigious North Miami Beach. There was a pool and jacuzzi on the top floor, an Oceanview balcony, and the beach was a ten-minute walk away.

During my time there, I prayed and asked God to give me a business connection so that I can claim a godly inheritance in my birth city.

That trip sparked eight months of travel for my family, and we traveled more places during that time frame than I did over the past 5 ½ years of our marriage. My kid's faith pushed me to create memorable experiences for them. Our escapades lightened the encumbering stress that caused me to skip meals and nearly faint in front of my students due to low blood sugar during my first week of teaching. On Labor Day, we visited WonderWorks and the Hollywood Wax Museum in Myrtle Beach. On our wedding anniversary, Sept 18, I visited Atlanta for the first time in 36 years, and we explored the Martin Luther King National Historic Park and the King Center. During the winter break, we revisited Atlanta so that my son could receive keloid removal surgery. This enabled him to no longer endure the teasing that I experienced as a child due to my keloids. We visited the Coca Cola Museum the day before my birthday, and I finally felt like I was living my best life for a change.

The trip of a lifetime came less than a week before I actually planned it. I had joined an incredible network marketing company, known as Financial Education Services. Our company allows me to get my credit fixed for free while making extra money.

After my mentor's husband tagged me in a social media post, I found the company requesting people who were interested in working from home. This opportunity allowed me the ability to create my own schedule as a referral agent. My mentor is one of our Vice Presidents, who joined our company after being fired from her job the week before her mother's funeral. One of our Senior Vice Presidents and Regional Sales Directors fervently urged me to catapult my training to the next level by attending our annual business convention. I passionately requested my husband treat our family to a Valentine's Day trip to Nevada. This trip changed our life.

We drove through ten states and traveled through several landforms and types of weather. The hills of Alabama were a pleasant surprise. The rain gushed down the sides of the hills like a waterfall. The huge windmills we saw along major highways were captivating, and the large cross showed me everything is definitely bigger in Texas. The red mountains of New Mexico, the gorgeous Grand Canyon, and the majestic snow-peaked mountains in Arizona made me realize that a trip to Las Vegas was a small feat in comparison to God's creation of these majestic mountain ranges. When we stopped to take a photo in Albuquerque, my son said, "Those mountains look like a picture! I can't believe it's real!" My daughter gazed in awe at the fancy big city lights in Las Vegas, and in those moments, I realized she is a city girl like me. As they walked to the arcade in Bally's Casino, while I attended business training sessions, they marveled at how grownups were playing what looked like substantial video games.

Each trip this past year confirmed my decision to make my own schedule like a boss instead of denying the encumbering stress of teacher burnout. And unfortunately, every trip caused my husband and I to grow farther and farther apart. Two weeks after the quarantine began, we experienced a 2.4 earthquake in Summerville, SC. Little did I know I would experience another quake in my heart two weeks later. I was asking my husband to help me recruit customers and give financial support to our next business conference in Orlando. He told me he wanted a divorce. I was finally feeling happier than I have ever been to. Still, he was feeling more incapable of supporting me and thought he could never give me the exotic trips I dreamed of.

The joy on my kid's faces during these zestful quests is priceless. I love giving my children what they desire because they are kind, funny, and smart kids. Right now, they want a condo with a Miami pool, just like the condo we visited this past summer. And I want that too.

What's the next city on the tiny travel agents' itinerary? They exclaimed, "Paris!" when I asked for their "after corona" plans. Jasmine said, "I want to go taste the macaroons!" and I gave her a puzzled look because I have never tasted that pastry, let alone knew what it meant. "And I always want to see the Eiffel Tower!" William said, which makes sense due to his fascination with architecture. Little do they know, I am making plans for them to go to Disney while I am at my conference in Orlando. The last time I was in Orlando was Grad Nite 2002, and it will be so sweet to revisit the city with my kids. I am amazed by the traveling opportunities I have as an entrepreneur, and I look forward to visiting and giving them the world. At the same time, I will continue to build the empire that I am creating for them.

About the Author:

Hazel Elaina taught elementary music, special education, and general education for twelve years in Florida and South Carolina. She was born and raised in Miami, Florida, and enjoys singing and playing the piano. She received a Bachelor's degree in Music Education from Florida International University. She obtained her Master's Degree in Special Education from Grand Canyon University. Her eight-year-old daughter Jasmine loves to read, and her nine-year-old son William loves science. She is a passionate network marketing entrepreneur who helps families become more debt-free through financial literacy.

Facebook: Hazel Elaina
Facebook Business: Hazel the Credit Consultant
Instagram: @hazelelaina_
Twitter: Hazel Elaina
Linked In: Hazel Elaina

A FINAL NOTE FROM THE PUBLISHER OF PURPOSE

#jesuscoffeeandprayer

BOSS MOM!

I Speak life over you on this day.

My full prayer is that you were encouraged, inspired, challenged, and motivated to walk into Your GREATER in Jesus Christ!

If the Boss Moms that you just heard from can do it~ Queen- So-Can- YOU!

Now Queen, if you read these inspirational stories and still feel lost, less than, and inadequate to run your race; then I'd like to introduce you to my Lord and Savior, Jesus Christ.

He is the fiber of my being and quite frankly- yours too.

You may not fully realize the Power that lies within you...But I am a living witness Queen, It lives within you- through HIM!

I invite you to say this quick yet life-changing prayer with me to accept Christ into Your life for the very 1st time or to simply renew your commitment.

If you feel lead, please read the below aloud:

Read Aloud & Believe in Your Heart

Heavenly Father,
I come to you now as humble as I know-how.
I recognize that I am broken- in more ways than one. I need
you, Lord, and I receive you on this day!
I am a sinner in need of a Savior.
I know that Jesus, you are that Savior.
You are the Son of God.
I know that you died for my sins and rose again on the 3rd
day to give me life.
I ask for your forgiveness, your love, and embrace now.
I repent from my sins and will follow you for the rest of my
life.
Make me new on this day, Lord.
I believe it, receive it and know that it is done!
In the Mighty Name of Jesus Christ, I pray all these things.
Amen!

Queen, if you said the above statement aloud and believed in your heart, I CELEBRATE and WELCOME You into the Body of Christ!

The bible tells us clearly:

If you declare with your mouth, "Jesus is Lord," and believe in your heart that God raised him from the dead, you will be saved. Romans 10:9 NIV

Queen, I encourage you to find a good bible-based church or community of believers who can support your journey along the way.

Know that Jesus loves you, and so do I!

You are my Sister in the body of Christ.

If you gave your life to Christ after reading this prayer, we want to know.

Please email us at <u>jesuscoffeeandprayer@gmail.com</u>

Be sure to put: SAVED in the subject line, and I will personally reach out to you!

May God bless you, richly for your Obedience- Welcome to the BOSS MOMS community of believers!

To God Be the Glory for Ever and Ever!

****

READY TO TAKE THE LEAP OF FAITH AND BECOME
A BEST-SELLING QUEEN CO-AUTHOR TOO!

VISIT WWW.JESUSCOFFEEANDPRAYER.COM
NOW FOR YOUR NEXT OPPORTUNITY

SCHEDULE YOUR FREE 20MIN. BEST-SELLING BOOK
CONSULTATION TODAY
JUST MENTION PROMO CODE: BOSS MOMS WHEN
YOU SUBMIT YOUR REQUEST!

BOSS MOMS REFLECT

Queen, I challenge you to take a moment to reflect on your hopes, your dreams, and the Calling over your life.

In the next few pages, Take a real moment to answer these thought-provoking questions. My hope is to propel you into an even GREATER YOU!

For a Full BOSS MOMS matching Journal/Planner- Visit www.jesuscoffeeandprayer to grab your copy!

How will you be a Boss Mom today?

_____

_____

_____

_____

_____

_____

_____

_____

_____

_____

_____

_____

_____

_____

_____

_____

List 1 Boss Mom Goal That You Will CRUSH today?

_____

_____

_____

_____

_____

_____

_____

_____

_____

_____

_____

_____

_____

_____

How will YOU take care of You this Year?

_____

_____

_____

_____

_____

_____

_____

_____

_____

_____

_____

_____

_____

_____

Boss Moms, Who or What is Stopping You from Achieving Your Dreams? / How will you Change that?

_____

_____

_____

_____

_____

_____

_____

_____

_____

_____

_____

_____

_____

_____

_____

_____

Everybody needs somebody Queen. You were Not designed to do it Alone. Name 3 Human beings that You can Count on!

_____

_____

_____

_____

_____

_____

_____

_____

_____

_____

_____

_____

_____

List 1 Boss Mom Goal You Will CRUSH This week?

_____

_____

_____

_____

_____

_____

_____

_____

_____

_____

_____

_____

_____

_____

How can you show your children (young or older) love today?

_____

_____

_____

_____

_____

_____

_____

_____

_____

_____

_____

_____

_____

_____

_____

_____

Boss Mom, What Will You Do Today to Grow Your Faith?

What are You willing to learn to Grow Your Business & Your Brand?

_____

_____

_____

_____

_____

_____

_____

_____

_____

_____

_____

_____

_____

List 1 Boss Mom Goal You Will CRUSH this month?

_____

_____

_____

_____

_____

_____

_____

_____

_____

_____

_____

_____

_____

_____

_____

How are you currently investing your time, effort, money and energy?

_____

_____

_____

_____

_____

_____

_____

_____

_____

_____

_____

_____

_____

List the 5 most important things in your life right now. Prioritize them. Now take a moment to Be TRUE to YOU and ask yourself: AM I Giving these listed items the attention/love they deserve?

_____

_____

_____

_____

_____

_____

_____

_____

_____

_____

_____

_____

_____

_____

Lord Willing, 1 Year from Now, where will you be? (Physically, Emotionally, Mentally, Spiritually, Financially- think family/kids too) Pour it Out Queen!

_____

_____

_____

_____

_____

_____

_____

_____

_____

_____

_____

_____

_____

_____

List 1 Boss Mom Goal You Will CRUSH this year?

_____

_____

_____

_____

_____

_____

_____

_____

_____

_____

_____

_____

_____

_____

_____

Finish this sentence Boss Mom:

If I am being completely honest with myself, I could really use help with: _____

Finish this sentence Boss Mom:

I WILL _____ in the Next 30 Days! #NoExcuses

Finish this Statement Boss Mom:

My Name is_____ and I AM WORTHY OF LOVE, GOOD HEALTH, & SUCCESS!

REPEAT AFTER ME QUEEN:
(SAY IT ALOUD-SAY IT LIKE YOU MEAN IT!)

I AM A WINNER

I AM VICTORIOUS

I AM BLESSED

NOW QUEEN, CREATE YOUR OWN BOSS MOMS AFFIRMATION STATEMENT:

YOU+POSITIVE+ I AM/ I WILL STATEMENT

*EX. I AM ENOUGH! ***No Cheating Queen- Create Your Own & OWN IT! *

Thank you!

www.ingramcontent.com/pod-product-compliance
Lightning Source LLC
Chambersburg PA
CBHW071515200326

41519CB00019B/5949

9 7 8 1 9 5 2 2 7 3 0 3 2